STEM *trailblazer* BIOS

ASTRONAUT
ELLEN OCHOA

HEATHER E. SCHWARTZ

Lerner Publications • Minneapolis

Lerner Publications Company
A division of Lerner Publishing Group, Inc.
241 First Avenue North
Minneapolis, MN 55401 USA

For reading levels and more information, look up this title at www.lernerbooks.com.

Content Consultant: James A. Flaten, Associate Director, NASA's Minnesota Space Grant Consortium

Library of Congress Cataloging-in-Publication Data

Names: Schwartz, Heather E.
Title: Astronaut Ellen Ochoa / by Heather E. Schwartz.
Description: Minneapolis : Lerner Publications, [2018] | Series: STEM trailblazer bios | Audience:
    Age 7-11. | Audience: Grade 4 to 6. | Includes bibliographical references and index.
Identifiers: LCCN 2016055016 (print) | LCCN 2017006235 (ebook) | ISBN 9781512434491 (lb : alk.
    paper) | ISBN 9781512456271 (pb : alk. paper) | ISBN 9781512451016 (eb pdf)
Subjects: LCSH: Ochoa, Ellen—Juvenile literature. | Women astronauts—United States—
    Biography—Juvenile literature. | Astronauts—United States—Biography—Juvenile literature. |
    Women scientists—United States—Biography—Juvenile literature. | Hispanic American women—
    Biography—Juvenile literature.
Classification: LCC TL789.85.O25 S39 2018 (print) | LCC TL789.85.O25 (ebook) | DDC
    629.450092 [B]—dc23

LC record available at https://lccn.loc.gov/2016055016

Manufactured in the United States of America
1-42098-25392-2/8/2017

The images in this book are used with the permission of: NASA/JSC, pp. 4, 6, 17, 21–25; Ashly Covington/Alamy Stock Photo, p. 8; Hans Blossey/Alamy Stock Photo, p. 10; Randy Montoya /Sandia National Laboratories, p. 12; © Smith Collection/Gado/Archive Photos/Getty Images, p. 14; © NASA/Handout/Hulton Archive/Getty Images, p. 15; NG Images/Alamy Stock Photo, p. 16; © NASA/Handout/Hulton Archive/Getty Images, p. 18; © NASA/Handout/Getty Images Sport/Getty Images, p. 19; NASA/Sipa USA/Newscom, p. 27.

Cover: NASA/JSC.

Main body text set in Adrianna Regular 13/22. Typeface provided by Chank.

CONTENTS

Chapter 1

Ellen Ochoa views Earth from a window on the International Space Station.

EXPLORING HER INTERESTS

When Ellen Ochoa was young, girls did not grow up to be astronauts. Ellen was interested in science, but she did not expect to travel to outer space as an adult.

Yet as the world changed around Ellen, so did her dreams.

And she surprised everyone by becoming the first female Hispanic American astronaut in 1991. She went on to log nearly one thousand hours in outer space.

EARLY IMPRESSIONS

Ellen was born on May 10, 1958, in Los Angeles, California. She spent her childhood near San Diego, California. Her father, Joseph, was Mexican American and ran a retail store. Her mother, Rosanne, was a homemaker. The family also included Ellen's sister and three brothers. Ellen was the middle child.

By fifth grade, Ellen thought she might like to be president of the United States one day. But she had many other interests and did not stick with that goal. She learned to play the flute.

TECH TALK

"I was definitely interested in space exploration when I was little, and the Apollo program was going on when I was in elementary and junior high. But at that time women were excluded from becoming astronauts, so I never thought it was a career I could grow up and pursue."

—*Ellen Ochoa*

Ochoa has continued playing the flute throughout her life.

She also liked math and science. In 1969, when Ellen was eleven, the Apollo 11 mission landed American astronauts on the moon. The moon landing made a big impression on Ellen. Along with the rest of the country, Ellen followed the news about this major historical event. But it didn't figure into her personal goals. Everyone knew all astronauts were men.

SMART FROM THE START

Ellen's parents divorced when she was a teenager. Ellen and her siblings lived with their mother and witnessed her determination as she took college classes part-time while working to support her family. It took Rosanne twenty-two years to earn her college degree. She expected the same perseverance and hard work from her children.

Ellen was a serious student throughout high school. She took **calculus** classes and was very interested in science and math. Some of her classmates thought that was strange for a girl. Some of her teachers thought so too.

In 1975, Ellen graduated from Grossmont High School in La Mesa, California. Her grades put her at the top of the class. She was named valedictorian, and she earned a four-year **scholarship** to Stanford University. She was not entirely sure what her career path would be. But her childhood and her education had prepared her for future success.

Chapter 2

San Diego
State University

FINDING FOCUS

Ellen was offered a scholarship to Stanford, but she chose to go to San Diego State University instead. It was closer to her family. Two of her brothers were still in high school, and she did not want to leave them behind.

At first, Ellen wasn't sure what she wanted her major area of study to be in college. At one time, she thought she might major in music. Business was another option. She also studied journalism and took a lot of math classes. She sped through the calculus classes many of her classmates saw as a burden. She thought they were fun.

Ellen considered majoring in **engineering**, but a professor discouraged her. He made it clear that it was not the right field for her because she was a woman. Finally, Ellen tried a **physics** class. She loved it. Her professors were encouraging, and they helped her see what she could do with a physics degree.

Ellen chose physics as her major and began to work even harder to pursue science. She even spent her summers studying science. During her breaks, she worked at Los Alamos National Laboratory, a lab that works to protect the United States from nuclear threats. The lab makes great advances in science and technology by studying how atoms behave in various situations. Even though Ellen was focused on physics, she did not give up on her other interests. She found music was a satisfying break from science and continued playing the flute.

LIGHTBULB MOMENT

Ochoa graduated from San Diego State University in 1980. She was valedictorian of her class once again, and she earned an engineering **fellowship** at Stanford University. This gave her financial assistance to continue her studies in graduate school, where students earn master's degrees and sometimes PhD degrees, or doctorates.

At Stanford, Ochoa majored in electrical engineering. She also kept studying physics. She focused her research on **optics** and worked to develop systems that help computers gather

Stanford University

WOMEN IN SPACE

NASA's astronaut training program started accepting female candidates in 1978. Six women were selected, and they completed the program a year later. In 1983, Sally Ride was the first American woman to travel into outer space.

information about objects from images. Her research led to the invention of an optical inspection system. It was used to prevent problems in the manufacturing of machine parts. Ochoa **patented** the invention. Eventually she earned both a master's degree and a doctorate in electrical engineering.

As a graduate student, Ochoa made some new connections. She met students who were working to get into the National Aeronautics and Space Administration (NASA) astronaut training program. When she realized that she was qualified for the program, Ochoa decided to apply too.

Chapter 3

At Sandia National Laboratories, scientists and engineers work to research and develop safe and environmentally friendly technologies.

LAUNCHING
HER CAREER

In 1985, Ochoa graduated from Stanford and applied for the astronaut training program. She did not get into the program the first time she applied. She did not get in the second time either.

Meanwhile, Ochoa started her career. Naturally, she went into the field that was her passion: engineering. Ochoa took a job as a research engineer at Sandia National Laboratories in Livermore, California. She continued the work she had started at Stanford and helped invent two more optical devices. Then she was listed on two more patents. She was making a name for herself in her field. She was becoming known as an expert and an inventor.

The third time Ochoa applied for the astronaut training program, NASA's scientists and engineers took notice. They saw that her work could be valuable for outer space missions. In 1987, Ochoa got some exciting news. She was one of one hundred finalists for the program.

LEARNING TO FLY

Ochoa picked up a new hobby while waiting to get into the astronaut training program. She got her private pilot's license. She knew it would be useful to understand flight as she worked toward becoming an astronaut.

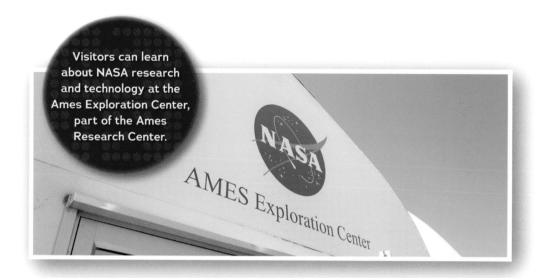

Visitors can learn about NASA research and technology at the Ames Exploration Center, part of the Ames Research Center.

JOINING NASA

In 1988, NASA hired Ochoa as a research engineer at the Ames Research Center in California's Silicon Valley. She soon became chief of the Intelligent Systems Technology Branch. She supervised thirty-five engineers and scientists. Her team worked on research and development for new systems and technology. They worked on optical and computer systems and designed technology that could be used in **aerospace** missions.

Ochoa was still working for NASA in 1990. That year, she learned her career was taking a dramatic new turn. She had been selected for NASA's astronaut training program.

None of Ochoa's Stanford friends made it in with her. She had achieved a dream few women had before her. There was plenty of work ahead, but Ochoa was elated. She knew her life would never be the same.

Ochoa practices using a parachute during her astronaut training.

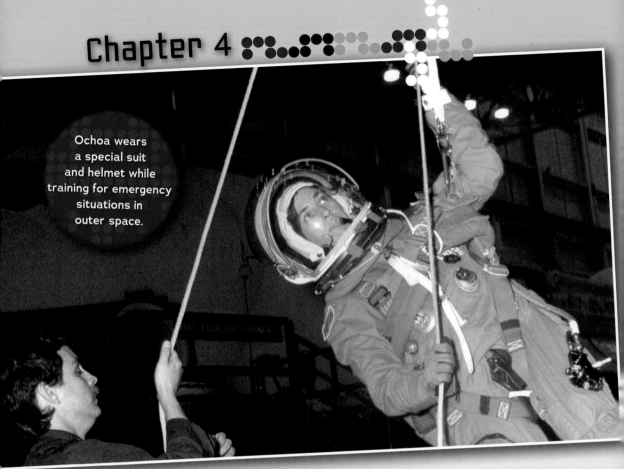

Chapter 4

Ochoa wears a special suit and helmet while training for emergency situations in outer space.

AIMING HIGH

As an astronaut in training, Ochoa had to move far from her home state of California. She left the Ames Research Center and went to the Johnson Space Center in Houston, Texas. Training to be an astronaut was intense. Ochoa had already earned several academic degrees. But there were more classes and tests to take. She needed to prove she had what it took to be an astronaut. She had to prove she was up to every challenge. Ochoa took more science classes. She studied outer space, Earth, the oceans, and the science of weather. She also took classes in first aid and survival techniques. Ochoa even took scuba diving classes to prepare for space walks. The feeling of being underwater is similar to weightlessness in space, so NASA trains its astronauts in a huge pool. Ochoa was tested on her knowledge of how a space shuttle worked. She had to understand every system on the shuttle and be prepared to handle anything she might encounter in outer space.

Ochoa participates in emergency training in the NASA training pool.

In 1991, Ochoa finished the training program. She was
officially an astronaut! But that did not mean she would be
going into outer space yet. First, she would be a flight software
specialist. This work involved developing, testing, and training
the robotic machines that would be used for missions in
space. She enjoyed the work. And she was not expecting to
leave Earth anytime soon. She knew that many astronauts
had to wait ten to sixteen years before they first traveled to

outer space. Yet for Ochoa, things ended up unfolding a little differently. It wasn't long before Ochoa was chosen to go on her first mission. She could hardly believe it. Just two years after completing astronaut training she would be on a mission to outer space.

STARTING A FAMILY

Ochoa's personal life took off in a new direction around the same time as her career did. In 1990, Ochoa married Coe Fulmer Miles, a computer research engineer. They have two sons.

Ellen Ochoa holds her son Wilson Miles-Ochoa.

ON A MISSION

In 1993, Ochoa boarded the space shuttle *Discovery* with four other astronauts. She was the only female on the crew. She was also the first Hispanic woman to travel into outer space. She was making history just by being herself.

The mission was nine days long. Ochoa's job was to do research on solar activity. She operated a 50-foot (15-meter) robotic arm called the Remote Manipulator System (RMS). She used the robotic arm to grab a satellite. The satellite was gathering **data** about the **solar corona**.

The work was challenging, and Ochoa loved it. She loved the view of Earth from space too. Her home planet looked beautiful and familiar. She later described it as looking the way it looks in movies about space but with much brighter colors.

Discovery launches to begin a mission in space.

Chapter 5

Ochoa poses with the *Atlantis* crew before their 1994 mission.

MILESTONE
MOMENTS

Ochoa continued flying on shuttle missions into outer space during the next nine years. The RMS played a big role in her work. Her second mission was in 1994 aboard the space shuttle *Atlantis*. Ochoa's job was similar to the one she'd had during her first mission. She collected more data about solar activity.

In 1999, Ochoa boarded the space shuttle *Discovery* again. This mission took her to the International Space Station (ISS). Another crew was planning to live there the next year, so Ochoa's crew had to deliver supplies for them ahead of time. This was the first time a space shuttle docked with the ISS.

In 1999, *Discovery* and its crew became the first orbiter and crew to dock with the International Space Station.

Ochoa floats through the tunnel that connected *Discovery* to the ISS.

On this mission, Ochoa also used the RMS to deliver parts and tools that would be used in future missions. She helped her crew during their eight-hour space walk to attach the parts and tools to the outside of the ISS. Ochoa later said using the RMS was challenging. The heavy supplies appeared to be weightless in orbit, but their mass made them awkward to move from the space shuttle to the ISS.

Ochoa poses for a NASA portrait before a shuttle mission.

TECH TALK

"We were driving in the car one day and we were passing Johnson Space Center and my son was in the back seat. I think he was about five. And he said, 'Mom, can boys be astronauts or just girls?'"

—Ellen Ochoa

In 2002, Ochoa returned to the ISS. She boarded the *Atlantis* for a second time. And this time, instead of using the RMS to move supplies, she moved crew members during their space walks. It was the first time the robotic arm was used in that way. Ochoa flew on four space shuttle missions total and spent nearly one thousand hours in outer space.

ENCOURAGING OTHERS

When Ochoa was not flying shuttle missions, she did important jobs for NASA on the ground. Sometimes she was in Mission Control, communicating with crews and supporting their missions in outer space. In 2013, she became director of the Johnson Space Center, the home of NASA's space program. Ochoa is the first Hispanic and second female to hold the position. She has also won many awards for her work and her service. She even has four schools named after her.

Along with her busy schedule at the Johnson Space Center, Ochoa visits schools to talk to students. She encourages girls, in particular, to work toward jobs in science and engineering. She also still believes that exploring other interests has many rewards. In her opinion, some of the best candidates

Ochoa speaks during a 2016 news conference.

SAFETY IN SPACE

In 2003, the space shuttle *Columbia* exploded. Ochoa was working in Mission Control for the first time that day. She later became part of a team that worked to make space missions both safer and more successful.

for NASA's astronaut training program do just that. They play sports. They study music. They learn foreign languages. Ochoa believes it is important to be involved and interested in lots of different areas. She is an astronaut who excels in many areas herself, and she is sure to continue contributing to NASA's work on Earth and in outer space.

TIMELINE

1958
Ellen is born.

1978
NASA's astronaut training program begins accepting women.

1979
The first female astronauts complete their NASA training.

1983
Sally Ride is the first American woman to travel into outer space.

1986
Franklin Chang Diaz becomes the first Hispanic American to go into outer space.

1988
NASA hires Ochoa.

1990
Ochoa is selected for NASA's astronaut training program.

1993
Ochoa becomes the first Hispanic woman on a mission to outer space.

2003
The space shuttle *Columbia* explodes.

2013
Ochoa becomes the first Hispanic and second female director of the Johnson Space Center.

2015
Ochoa receives the National Space Grant Distinguished Service Award for her service to the space program.

SOURCE NOTES

5 Ellen Ochoa, "Preflight Interview: Ellen Ochoa," NASA, accessed November 21, 2016, http://spaceflight.nasa.gov/shuttle/archives/sts-96/crew/intochoa.html.

26 Ellen Ochoa, "Makers Profile: Ellen Ochoa," Makers.com, accessed November 21, 2016, http://www.makers.com/ellen-ochoa.

GLOSSARY

aerospace
dealing with travel in and above Earth's atmosphere

calculus
an advanced branch of mathematics

data
facts and information used to calculate and analyze something

engineering
the work of designing and creating new products and systems using scientific methods

fellowship
money given to a graduate student who teaches or does research at a university

optics
the science that studies light and the way it affects and is affected by matter

patented
protected by an official document that gives a person or company the right to be the only one that makes or sells a product for a certain period of time

physics
a science that deals with motion and properties of matter, forces, energy, and waves

scholarship
an amount of money given by a school or other organization to help a student pay for his or her education

solar corona
the ultrahot region surrounding the sun

BOOKS

Di Piazza, Domenica. *Space Engineer and Scientist Margaret Hamilton*. Minneapolis: Lerner Publications, 2018. Read about another woman who helped pave the way for space exploration and women in science.

Schwartz, Heather E. *NASA Mathematician Katherine Johnson*. Minneapolis: Lerner Publications, 2018. Learn about a woman who worked behind the scenes to help make the first US mission to space possible.

Stine, Megan. *Who Was Sally Ride?* New York: Grosset & Dunlap, 2013. Find out about the first American woman astronaut to travel to outer space.

WEBSITES

Easy Science for Kids: Famous Woman Scientists
http://easyscienceforkids.com/famous-women-scientists -video-for-kids
Find out more about important women who studied science.

NASA for Students
https://www.nasa.gov/audience/forstudents/k-4/index.html
Learn more about NASA, astronauts, and the International Space Station.

NASA Kids' Club
https://www.nasa.gov/kidsclub/index.html
Play games and learn more about NASA's work.

LERNER

SOURCE™

Expand learning beyond the printed book. Download free, complementary educational resources for this book from our website, www.lerneresource.com.

INDEX

ABOUT THE AUTHOR

Heather E. Schwartz has written more than sixty nonfiction books for kids. She always enjoys researching and learning about people with a passion for what they do, such as Ellen Ochoa.